MIGRATING SUCCESSFULLY TO

WATER BASED ADHESIVES

Unlocking the Mystery of Prefect Sole attaching & Pre-Treatments

MIGRATING SUCCESSFULLY TO

WATER BASED ADHESIVES

Unlocking the Mystery of Prefect Sole attaching & Pre-Treatments

AMIT BAJORIA

Worldwide Published by
Pendown Press

PENDOWN PRESS

An ISO 9001 & ISO 14001 Certified Co.,

Regd. Office: 2525/193, 1st Floor, Onkar Nagar-A,
Tri Nagar, Delhi-110035

Ph.: 09350849407, 09312235086

E-mail: info@pendownpress.com

Branch Office: 1A/2A, 20, Hari Sadan, Ansari Road,
Daryaganj, New Delhi-110002

Ph.: 011-45794768

Website: PendownPress.com

First Edition: 2020

Price: ₹4,80,000/-

ISBN: 978-93-90479-94-8

Layout and Cover Designed by Pendown Graphics Team

Printed and Bound in India by Thomson Press India Ltd.

I would like to dedicate
this book to my all my family members,
entire SKICORP team,
Mr. Luca & Mr. Paolo Giugni
who have given me immense support
and helped me become the version
of the man I am today.

Table of Contents

Preface

In my fascinating experience of getting factories migrate From Solvent adhesives to Water based adhesives we have always encountered the secret desire of Footwear Factories who want to migrate form solvent adhesives to water based adhesives. This desire is fuelled by various reason like:

- Have a more safer productions and eliminating risk of Fire Hazards in productions
- Making the factories more safe by eliminating free flowing toxic solvents in air. Thus making the production place more health friendly for everyone inside the factories.
- Making the footwear production more eco friendly and reducing the pollution caused due to solvent adhesives.
- Meeting the ever increasing expectations of the brands & buyers particularly related to compliances.
- Reducing the cost & reducing the manpower requirements by finding easier way to apply adhesives.

In early stages of my career I was extremely delighted to see such strong will to move to newest greener technologies of Bonding soles. Over period of time I realised the biggest gap between the Desire & the reality. This was also driven by the lack of real intent which was triggered by extremely poor Knowledge of the subject. Furthermore too much scattered information's and often misleading resulted in a lot of factories not able to migrate or only partially able to migrate to WATER Based Adhesives For Sole Bonding. That's why I decided to write this book. It was very important to give complete overview & a detailed clarity of challenges , Identification of materials/ substrates, complete process, Control mechanism, Test methods & compliance requirements.

The purpose of writing this book is to make readers understand that if followed the right knowledge , product & process it possible to migrate to Water Based Adhesives for Sole Bonding in a short span of time.

Understand this: the only way we can successfully migrate sole bonding ion water based if we following the complete Bonding technology. Any shortcuts can lead to big disasters and hence very important to follow every chapter of the book carefully.

Writing this book has been a challenge and there were days when I wanted to give up this idea of writing this book, only to realize that the essence of this book itself is to persist and that is what I continued to nurture. This journey of writing a book has helped me discover the deeper layers on the subject and made me grow as a person.

I invite you to share these tools & techniques with me through this book and nurture the skills to become a winner.

This is not just a book. This is your practical guide to set you to successfully migrate to Water based adhesives avoiding big risk on the path of becoming a solvent free factory.

I eagerly look forward to hearing all your feedbacks and success.

Acknowledgements

This book is a product of my 25 years of experience. The book is a comprehensive guide for Migrating of Sole Bonding in footwear factory to water-based adhesives.

I would like to acknowledge all those who encouraged me to go deeper into my thoughts to bring those pearls out (get the book out of me!) that can serve millions.

I have had the opportunity to implement water-based adhesives to all the individual customers. I want to say thank you for being the inspiration and insight for me to get better with my techniques.

I am extending special gratitude to my Parents, my wife, my brother and all family members for they enabled me to lead this life with their incredible love and support. My team members also deserve special mention in this list.

A big thanks to my Mr Luca Giugni & Mr. Paolo Giugni who have always pushed me to Dream Big in life.

Last, but not least, thanks to all my mentors and teachers who have changed my life through their coaching, teaching, training, seminars, and mentoring programs.

01. Introduction

Sole attaching is the so called “kings discipline” because it needs a durable bonding. Let us look a little bit deeper in that subject and focus on sole attaching with water based adhesives.

Why water based (sole attaching) adhesives?

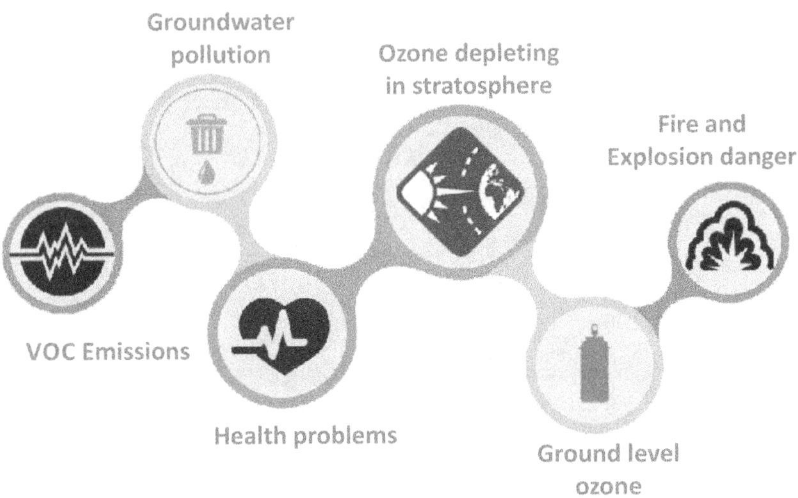

And..and..and..

02. Explanation of basic facts

It is necessary to know a little ABC of basic facts, connected to glues.

About this module

Module 2 will provide an overview about basic facts.

Learning target

- To get to know physical and chemical basic facts
- To be able to identify important basic facts and to widen the expertise

02. Explanation of basic facts

Fungi Resistance

Test to see how yeast, fungi, moulds etc. are growing on an adhesive film under a special "jungle" atmosphere.

1 – C adhesive

Single - component adhesive. This is an adhesive that cures under the influence of temperature, and as such requires no second component to be added. For that reason, 1 - C adhesives do not have to be mixed prior to application. A 1 - C adhesive is hence supplied in a single container.

2 – C adhesive

Two - component adhesive. This is an adhesive that has to be mixed with other substances in order to trigger its adhesive function. For that reason, 2 - C adhesives are supplied in at least 2 containers and in general must be mixed prior to application.

02. Explanation of basic facts

Activation
Effects of heat and suitable solvents, in order to renderdry adhesive films tacky again.

Activation Temperature
The temperature which must be achieved by exposure to infrared rays to render an adhesive film tacky again.

Activation Time
The time necessary to reach the temperature needed for activating the adhesive film.

Adhesion
Interfacial binding strength between the object to the bonded and the adhesive.

Aging Tests
Tests to see how durable a bond is after an aging process.

02. Explanation of basic facts

Application

Application or use of an adhesive during the bonding process.

Assembly line

Line for attaching shoe soles with shoe uppers.

Bonding technology

Summary of the bonding steps like, substrate preparation and pretreatment, drying times of primer and adhesives, heat activation, temperature, pressing time... Always released after preliminary tests.

02. Explanation of basic facts

Capped/ Capsulated Hardener

Cross linker based on Isocyanat already incorporated in a 1 component PUD adhesiveand not reacting at normal temperature.

Cohesion

Inside strength of the adhesive film or strength of the glue.

Contact bonding

After a drying time the dry adhesive films build up bonding with high strengths within a certain time (tack time) at lying together under pressure, which mostly further increase.

Creep resistance

The ability of an adhesive to be subjected to external forces over a longer period of time and not to be deformed or undergo very little deformation.

Creep tests

Test where a bond is loaded with weight at a higher temperature during 10 minutes. Test result is how large the bonded substrates have opened.

Dispersion

A fine distribution of solid, semi-solid or viscous substances in liquids which cannot dissolve them.

02. Explanation of basic facts

Emulsion
A fine distribution of liquid substances in liquids which cannot dissolve them.

EVA
ETHYLENE – VINYL ACETATE – COPOLYMER,
- linked/cured cross with peroxide as low density soling/midsole material in use.

Failure mode
Describes the reasons why a bonding failed or passed quality control.

Final strengths
Binding strengths after complete setting/crosslinking/drying/crystallizing of the adhesive. As a rule, 90% of final strengths is achieved after 24 hours.

02. Explanation of basic facts

Flash Point

The temperature where the vapour of a solvent or a solvent mixture may be ignited in the presence of air by sparks or a short action of an open flame. Self–ignition flash point is not the same.

Halogenating

Primering process for rubber

Hardener

Substances or mixtures of substances which are added to the adhesive before using, in order to effect the chemical curing of the adhesive. It is also called curing agent, crosslinking agent, catalyst, alkalinizing agent, etc.

Heat Activation Bonding

Bonding method, at which the glue causes a glue free non blocking adhesive film. At sufficient warming they become bondable and under pressure they connect with other adhesive films or materials, to reach a solid permanent bonding.

Heat Aging Test

Aging test on a bond under high temperature during 7 days in a heated chamber.

High viscous

Thick flowing

02. Explanation of basic facts

Hot tack LIFE	Describes the timeframe where the adhesive films are tacky when heat is activated. Must be long enough to enable spotting and pressing of the soles.
Hotmelts	Adhesive, that is used melted and builds up a solid adhesive layer at cooling down.
Hydrolysis aging test	Aging test of a bond under high temperature/high humidity during 7 days in a hydrolysis chamber.
Initial strengths	Tensile strengths, (maximum load that a material can support without fracture when being stretched), peel strengths the measure of the average **force** to part two bonded materials immediately after sole attaching.
Lamination	Joining layers of usually high-area, flexible substrates (e.g. films, fabrics) using an adhesive to form a laminate.

02. Explanation of basic facts

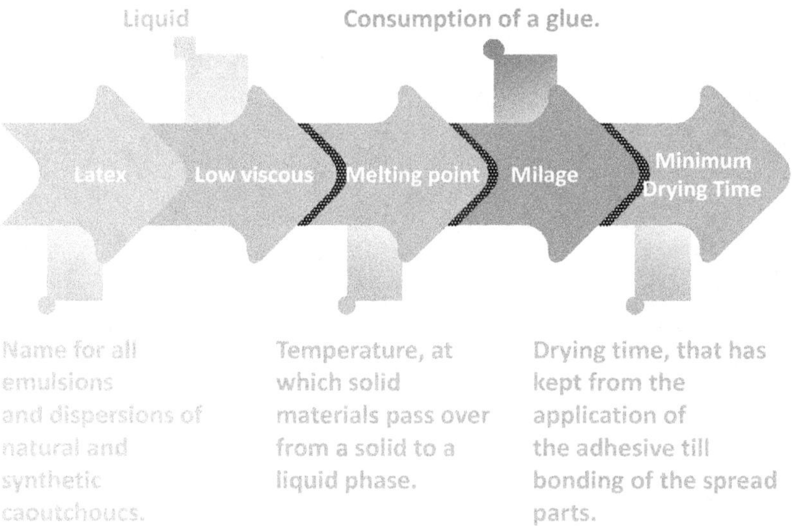

02. Explanation of basic facts

MSDS Material Safety Data Sheet.

PA Polyamide.

NBR Nitrile rubber, cured for oil and acid resistant soling materials.

NR Natural rubber (CREPE) from the Hevea Brasiliensis tree.

Open time Time, within a bonding is possible after application of an adhesive and observance of the minimum drying time.

02. Explanation of basic facts

Peel stress

Line-form stresses that only act on a line (e.g. removing / peeling off a film). The resistance of bonded joints to peel forces is determined using the floating roller peel test or T-peel test in accordance with DIN EN 1464. In the roller peel test, a brittle and a flexible substrate are required. In the T-peel test two flexible substrates are required. The tests are predominantly used for comparing adhesives and bonds as well as for monitoring the suitability of surface pretreatment methods (fracture pattern analysis).

Plasticizer

Term for inert liquid or solid organic substances having a low vapour pressure. Mainly esters by chemical nature. They physically interact with polymers (no chemical reaction), and are "softening" materials.

Pot Life

Time, within a reaction mixture of two or more materials can be processed.

Pressing Time

Recommended are 6 to 8 seconds minimum, in some cases where a very high initial strengths is requested longer/as long as possible.

Primers

Special formulations, which are applied to the newly treated surfaces. They improve the bondability of substrates to be bonded with an adhesive.

02. Explanation of basic facts

Pink stain test
Migration test

PP
Polypropylene

PVC
Polyvinyl Chloride

PMMA
Polymetacrylate

PS
Polystyrene

RUBBER
Abbreviation for all kinds of vulcanized (cured) rubber types like (NR, NBR, SBR, CR, ...).

PUD
Abbreviation for water based dispersion on PUR base.

PUR
Abbreviation for polyurethane. Important soling and upper material for shoes.

02. Explanation of basic facts

Release agent

Silicones, waxes, greases, oils, which prevent the bodies during the production.

Self life

Best before time. Timeframe for best quality.

Shear strength

This is the maximum shear stress, *i.e.* shearing force per unit surface area, which a bond can withstand.

Stock fitting line

Line for pretreatment/ manufacturing of soles.

Stresses on a bond

Describes the possible forces which can work on a bonded sole (see also graphic)

Substrates

Solid objects that are joined or have to be joined with each other.

02. Explanation of basic facts

Tack

Tackiness of the adhesive films in order to allow an easy spotting of the soles. We know a cold TACK and a hot tack after heat reactivation of the adhesive films.

TDS

Technical Data Sheet.

Tensile strength

The tensile strength gives the maximum tensile stress, namely tensile force per unit surface area, which a material or bond can withstand. The critical tensile stress results in fracture.

Test methods

Test methods are selected depending on the properties of the bonded joint under study.

02. Explanation of basic facts

Thixotropy

Description for the phenomenon whereby gels become liquid on applying mechanical forces (e.g. stirring, shaking, ultra - sound), but return to their original form again when the mechanical forces no longer act.

Workplace/ Threshold limit value

An independent bodyof experts has set down upper limits for exposure to a range of substances at the workplace (maximum workplace concentration). These limits particularly concern gases, volatile substances (present as vapours in ambient air), aerosols and dust.

Toxicology

It is the task of toxicology to study, recognize and assess the harmful effects of chemical substances or mixtures of chemical substances on life.

TPR (TR)

Thermoplastic rubber, soling material processed by thermoplastic injection moulding.

Viscosity

Name for thickness of an adhesive.

03. Identification of materials/substrates and requests on the bond

What kind of material substrate do we want to bond, what type of shoe is produced, what are the requests on aging properties....

About this module

Module 3 shall give you important information about the secure identification of the ground material of substrates used for shoe production. To know the material that we want to glue, is the only possibility to make a material specific pre-treatment correctly.

Learning target

- You should be able to recognize the substrate classes from various sole and shoe component materials.
- You are allowed to use different helping tools such as Bunsen burner, copper wire, dissolvent and other means.

03. Identification of materials/substrates and requests on the bond

Soling materials/uppers: Their use and possibilities to identify them

Footwear manufacturing is indeed a complex process. Its process involves transformation and assembly of a number of components made up of different materials. All these materials have a distinct role to play and all these materials contribute immensely to manufacture a shoe that is perfect shape and structure-wise.

In the footwear industry, a multitude of the most different materials are used. Their bondability differs highly due to their different chemical structure. This necessitates frequently an identification.

In most cased, this is quite complicated and requires experts in correspondingly equipped laboratories. Often, however, it will be enough to determine the synthetic group to which the material in question belongs.

The following information offers a survey of the synthetics, most frequently used in the footwear industry.

03. Explanation of basic facts

Polyurethane (PUR)
Soles made of integral skin foam, heels and plateau made from hard, cushions of soft foam, as well as top layers on synthetic upper and lining materials. Under the designation of TPU (thermoplastic polyurethane) also used for outsoles.

Polyvinyl Chloride (PVC)
Used for soles and heels, as top layer on synthetic upper material and linings in inserts.

Thermoplastic Rubber Based on Thermoplastic Rubber Based on Styrene Butadiene - Styrene (TR or TPR)
Mainly used for outsoles, but also for heels and plateau as well as foot beds.

Polystyrene (PS)
For heels and wedges.

03. Explanation of basic facts

Acrylonitrile-Butadiene-Styrene (so called Impact-Type Polystyrene) (ABS)

For heels, wedges and plateau white and easily colored.

Polypropylene and PET – Polyethylene (PP)

For ski boots. Very hard and flexible

Polymethyl-Methacrylate (PMMA)

As a sole material for plateau of fashionable ladies' shoes. Water

Ethylene-Vinyl Acetate-Copolymer (EVA)

Micro-Cellular for extremely light sole- and midsole material. Also used for plateau and heel wedges. Cross-linked with Peroxyde it became a Duroplast. For Plateau insoles a mix of eva /polyethylene is processed by Thermoplastic injection moulding.

03. Identification of materials/substrates and requests on the bond

Simple Methods for Identifying the Individual Plastics

PVC

Flame Test

Not flammable, flame goes out, melts entirely, very acrid smell of burning, in connection with a copper wire the flame assumes green color.

Solubility Properties

In tetrahydrofurane and cyclohexanone typical plastics characteristics, stiff and hard in cold

03. Identification of materials / substrates and requests on the bond

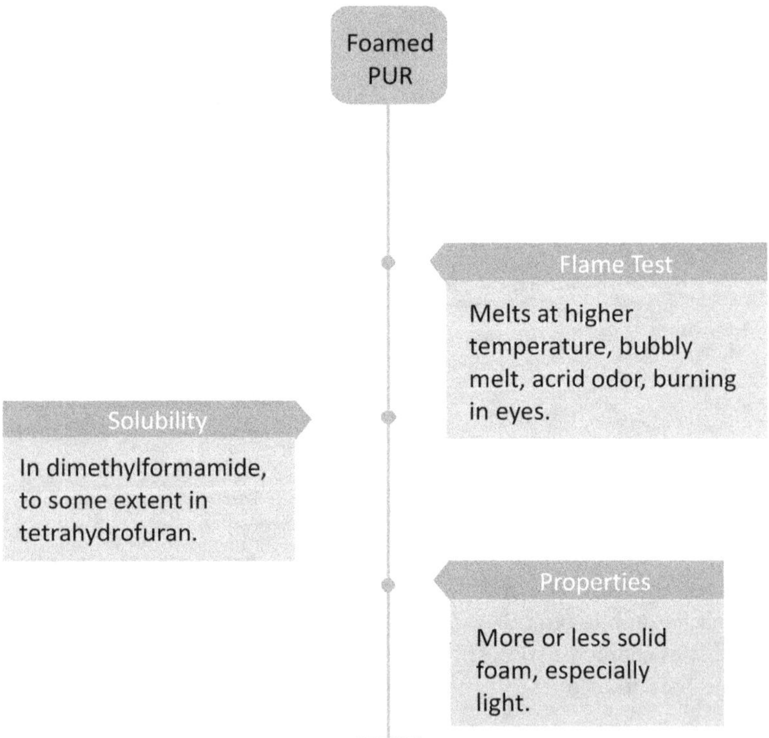

03. Identification of materials/substrates and requests on the bond

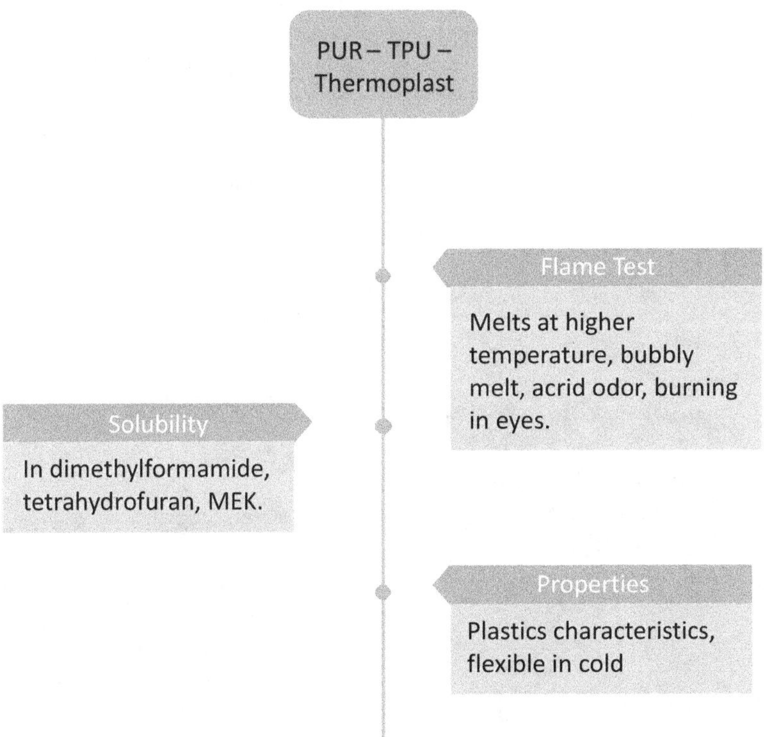

03. Identification of materials/substrates and requests on the bond

TPR– Thermoplastic Rubber

Flame Test

Burns with highly sooty flame, sweetish odor, melts easily

Solubility

In acetone, ethyl acetate, MEK, toluene and many other solvents, very easily soluble.

Properties

Very wide spectrum, may be fashioned in many ways, thereby may meet many requests for new fashions and styles.

03. Identification of materials/substrates and requests on the bond

PS–Polystyrene

Flame Test

Burns with high scooty flame, sweetish odor, melts easily.

Solubility

In acetone, ethyl acetate, MEK, toluene and many other solvents very easily soluble.

Properties

Typical plastics characteristics, metallic sound when struck.

03. Identification of materials/substrates and requests on the bond

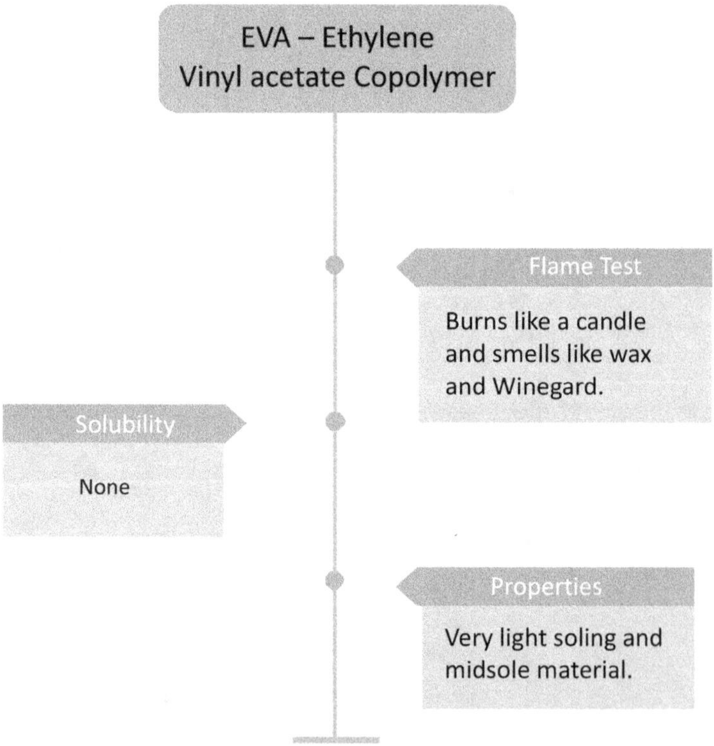

03. Identification of materials/substrates and requests on the bond

PA - POLYAMIDE

Flame Test

Smells like burned feathers or nails

Solubility

None

Properties

Very durable soles for soccer boots

03. Identification of materials / substrates and requests on the bond

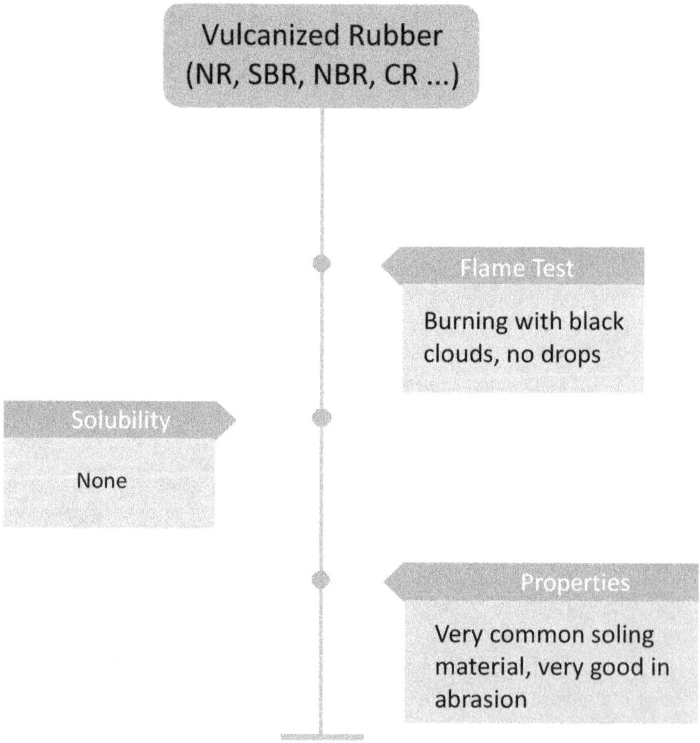

04. Different kinds of soling materials including bonding technologies

Let us consider the “kings discipline“, the sole attaching of the different kinds of soling materials. Module 4 gives an overview regarding bonding of the main substrates in use for soles. Pretreatment and final bonding are combined.

Learning targets

After Module 4, you should know how to bond:

- PUR soles
- Rubber soles
- Leather soles
- EVA soles
- PVC soles
- Stock fitted soles
- TPR soles
- CREPE soles
- PA soles

04. Different kinds of soling materials including bonding technologies

Bonding of the different kind of soles

1. Vulcanized rubber soles

Roughened and in some cases also unroughened soles can be bonded after treatment with a halogenating agent. The pretreatment process is called halogenating or chlorinating. The surface of the soles to be halogenated/bonded must be free of impurities like grease, dust, oil, paint and varnish coats and so on.

Halogenating can be done by brush or commercial available applicator machines. Minimum drying time and longest storing time of halogenated soles depends also on the substrates, as a rule, the drying should be 1 hour and 3 week storing of soles before further processing.

Halogenating method needs a Polyurethane adhesive for final bonding.

04. Different kinds of soling materials including bonding technologies

Bonding of the different kinds of soles

2. PUR soles

During the manufacture of such soles, release agents of various kinds are used. In order to remove the release agents and lacquers, it is recommended to roughen the soles before applying the adhesive. In individual cases it will be possible to prepare the soles for a bonding by cleaning them with a solvent and or using a Primer.

3. Croupon Leather soles

A roughening and opening the leather fibers for good adhesive penetration is the pretreatment target by mechanical roughening.

In case of wrong penetration of glues, a Primer can be applied as well. The technology of tanning and the grease content of the leather have to be considered.

04. Different kinds of soling materials including bonding technologies

Bonding of the different kinds of soles

4. EVA soles

EVA soles are cross-linked by peroxide and a roughening is possible. However, the use of a Primer is a common thing.

Worldwide is the largest use of EVA soles for athletic boot midsoles. The bonding is done by using a so called UV Primer. Cleaning, application of UV Primer and curing in an UV curing chamber is the common bonding way for pretreatment. The UV curing is done with UV-A and UV-B waves with an energy of 0,5-0,6 J/cm2. Final bonding with PUD's like ECOSTICK 18201 K.

4.1. EVA microcell, dye cut, unit soles... Bonding

After roughening or cut splitting a NON UV Primer is applied and finally bonded with PU adhesive.

04. Different kinds of soling materials including bonding technologies

Bonding of the different kinds of soles

4.2. Phylonbonding:

Phylon is a synonym and often used for CMEVA (compressed moulded EVA) and IMEVA (injection moulded EVA), mainly used as midsoles for Athletic Footwear.

The pretreatment steps, up to the final bonding with PU adhesives are:

- Cleaning by solvent wiping/cleaner wiping
- Application of UV Primer
- Curing of UV Primer in a curing chamber.

  CMEVA needs 0,5 J/cm2, IMEVA needs 0,7J/ cm2 Energy
- Final bonding with PU adhesive

04. Different kinds of soling materials including bonding technologies

Bonding of the different kinds of soles

5. PVC soles

Bonding is done by solvent wiping and using PU adhesive. Fresh PVC soles do not need solvent wiping, only during storing plasticizer etc. can be migrated to the surface and must be removed.

6. Stockfitted soles

Stock-fitted soles are made from different kinds of materials and from importance for the final bonding are the adhesives which are used and the pretreatment as well during stockfitting.

04. Different kinds of soling materials including bonding technologies

Bonding of the different kinds of soles

7. TPR (TR) soles:

For the bonding of soles based on SBS (styrene-butadiene-styrene) rubber, the halogenation will be taken into account in the first place. Care must be taken that the surface of the soles to bonded is free from all impurities. Rests of varnish, release agents, finished or dyed surfaces adversely affect their ability to halogenate. A roughening of the soles is not recommended and no means replace the halogenations. TPR is very sensitive to solvents

---

8. Natural rubber soles (CREPE)

The halogenating process is recommended for bonding. Halogenating and PU adhesive can also avoid problems with high oil containing crepe.

---

9. Summary of Pretreatment technologies for ECOSTICK

18201 K

---

04. Different kinds of soling materials including bonding technologies

Examples of typical materials with surface preparation are:

Material	Pretreatment/ cleaning	Halogenation/ Primer	Comments
Crepe (NR)	Cleaning with Heptane or mix Ethyl acetate/Heptane	Halogenation (=chlorination)	Don't use Benzene, is toxic and compliance letter banned
EVA phylon (IMEVA OR CMEVA)	Cleaning with different solvent mixes; also special cleaners with ingredients in use	UV primer	Primer needs a UV curing chamber
EVA dye cut (microcell)	Mainly no cleaning necessary	Non UV primer (solution of chlorinated PP in solvents)	
PVC	MEK(butanone)	None	MEK =Methyl Ethyl Ketone
PUR	MEK (butanone) Or roughening	None	Don' t use NEP + NMP! Are compliance banned and SVHC productsSVHC=Substances of very High Concern
Material	Pretreatment/ cleaning	Halogenation/ Primer	Comments
TPU	MEK (butanone)	None	
TPR (SBS)	Cleaning with Heptane Mainly no cleaning necessary	Halogenation	
Vulcanized Rubber filled (filled Rubber plates)	None	Halogenation	
Vulcanized Rubber unfilled/ Vulcanized transparent Rubber	Roughening	Halogenation	
Canvas	None	None	

05. Sole attaching manual

What should we consider when talking about sole attaching manual?

About this module

Module 5 shows us what technical things we have to consider when bonding soles.

Learning target

- How to attach the sole?
- Pressing properties
- Drying of WB adhesives
- Heat activation
- Upper preparation
- Cementing of soles

05. Sole attaching manual

Sole bonding manual

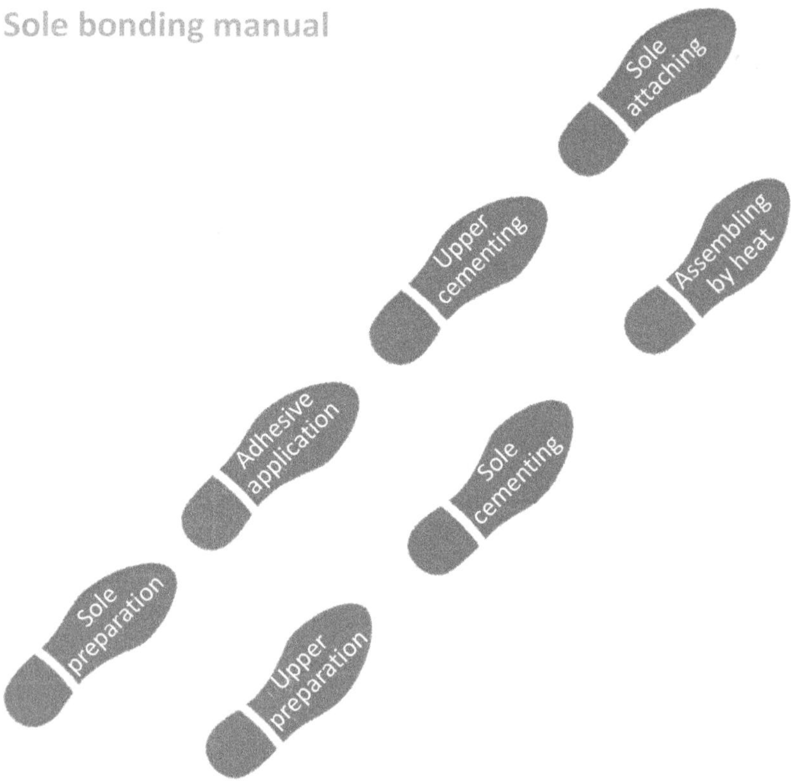

05. Sole attaching manual

Sole bonding manual

Sole preparation

- A material specific preparation has to be done.
- See Module 4 point 9
- Be aware on minimum drying time of the different Primers and the longest possible storing time of pretreated soles!

And a rule is

	Pretreatment	Minimum drying	Longest storing
PVC	Solvent wipe and dried	min. 20 min	1 day
Rubber	Roughen followed by Halogenation	Min. 45 min.	3 weeks
TPR	Halogenation	1 hour	1 week
EVA/ Phylon	Cleaner wipe Primer	20 min.	2 weeks
EVA/microell	Primer	30 min.	2 weeks
PUR	Rough or ... solvent wipe	- 15 min.	3 weeks 1 day

Minimum times are set at usual room temperature and can be shortened by using heat chambers etc.

05. Sole attaching manual

Sole bonding manual

Sole preparation

- Be aware that "ageing" effects may have taken place on soles stored for lengthy periods before use and so preparation will probably need to be more thorough than normal or an additional pretreatment step.
- Where there is a choice of roughing or solvent wiping (for example, as on PU sole units), the former is preferred easier.
- Avoid flooding or pudding primer.
- Store soles after priming with treated sides inwards to avoid cross contamination. Use canvas bags.

Halogenation Agent using:

- Pots and brushes should be free of metal.
- Be aware of best before time and keep away from strong light. • Avoid contamination in container/ pot.
- For TPR (TR) soles the use of a soft brush, for Rubber a stiff brush is recommended when applied by hand.
- Turn treated soles upside down to dry.

05. Sole attaching manual

Sole bonding manual

Upper preparation

- Lasting margin should be 8 mm minimum.
- Leather has to be roughened, in critical areas with high accuracy.
- Synthetics can be wiped with solvents or roughened. As a rule those preparations should be done which allow the highest bonding strengths.

05. Sole attaching manual

Sole bonding manual

Sole Cementing

- Apply an even coat and avoid "lakes."
- The adhesive needs to be dry or virtually dry before heat activation. The activation Step helps to finally dry the adhesive, especially in combined dryer/activator units. Although water-based adhesives may be white or translucent on application they dry, like solvent-based adhesives, to clear films. A clear film generally indicates that the adhesive is dry.

Upper cementing

- Apply the adhesive onto the material specific pretreated lasting margin and let them dry.

05. Sole attaching manual

Sole bonding manual

Assembling by heat activation

One and two way activation:

- If only sole is activated, the surface should reach a temperature of 80-90°C. With water-based adhesives the common practice of warming the upper at the same time is helpful. Similarly, two way activation of both sole and upper to 70°C gives good results. For our 1820 1 K adhesive we need a temperature of 70°C minimum in order to get started the cross-linking process of the capsulated cross linker in the adhesive.

- Note that overheating can be as bad for the sole bond as under heating. On thermoplastic rubbers, look for surface blistering during activation. If this occurs, the temperature is too high, the drying times too short or both. Also the TPR quality can be wrong or halogenating drying was too short.

- Activating relatively slowly over 10-15 seconds, especially with longer wavelength activator, rather than rapid flash activation for about 5 seconds, is generally beneficial in approving adhesion. Longer wavelength activators are also less sensitive to the color of the soling, allowing similar activation times to be used for mixed work. However, the correct activation time should always be determined.

05. Sole attaching manual

Sole bonding manual

Sole attaching

- Look for adequate heat activation temperature.
- Avoid delay between activation, spotting and pressing.
- The hot tack life of Ecostick 1820 1 K is excellent, but in case spotting tack problems occur, warm upper and sole also.
- A pressing time of minimum 8 seconds is recommended, in very hot areas prolongate pressing as long as possible.
- Check the correctness of press pad boxes by using indigo paper or satra pressure pack/ foil.

05. Sole attaching manual

Sole bonding manual

Others

- Check best before time of the glue
- Mix up the adhesive before using
- In case you add an additional outside hardener/crosslinker consider the POT LIFE of the mixture.

As a rule is valid:

- Pot life 1820 1 K + 4% crosslinker is 4 hours (HARDENER DN)
- After 4 hours you can add again 4% crosslinker when glue has not been used up. Again 4 hours pot life.
- After this period not used adhesive mix must be disposed.

06. Direct soling

About this module

In Module 6 we describe technologies for direct attachment of soling materials onto uppers.

Learning target

- You should know what kind of different direct attaching technologies are used.
- What kind of raw materials as soling materials are used
- For the direct attaching of soles are many of technologies available and also plenty of soling materials.

06. Direct soling

Frankly speaking we have 3 groups:

1. Direct attachment with thermoplastic compounds by extrusion (TPU, TPR, PVC).

2. Direct attachment of 2 component PUR (Injection, moulding and pouring on).

3. Direct attachment of Rubber mixtures by using injection moulding technology or attaching on in presses. The Rubber is vulcanized at high temperature.

In some cases, we do not need a glue for instance when 2 component PUR-foam is direct attached.

For all direct attachment technologies, we have suitable adhesion promoters available. The choice of adhesive is done according to the production technologies and of course according the used substrates.

07. Water based sole attaching glue

PUD-WATERBASED SOLE ATTACHING GLUE ECOSTICK 1820 1 K

One component and two component adhesives .....

About this module

The crosslinking of PUD's can be done with capped Isocyanates (we talk about one component adhesives), in that case Isocyanate is already incorporated in the adhesive....or the crosslinker can be added outside and have to be mixed and dispersed into the glue. In that case we are talking regarding 2 component glues.

Learning target

- Know the strength of one component web adhesives.
- Know the strength of two component adhesives.

07. Water based sole attaching glue

ECOSTICK 1 COMPONENT POLYURETHAN DISPERSION ADHESIVE WITH CAPPED

CROSSLINKER ECOSTICK 1820 1K

Is a single – component adhesive and solvent free.

Mixing of components prior to the application is thereof not necessary, hence the glue is supplied in a single container.

It is an adhesive that crosslinks under the influence of temperature and as such requires no second component to be added.

The crosslinking starts when temperature of >70°C is warming up the dried adhesive film during heat activation prior to spotting and pressing the soles.

The self life is up to 6 months from time of production.

07. Water based sole attaching glue

ECOSTICK 1820

In cases of highest requests on the durability of the bond it is also possible to add up to 4% outside crosslinker and to proceed as so-called 2 component adhesive. In that case, it has to be mixed with a hardener (crosslinker) for some minutes in order to ensure good dispersion of adhesive and hardener.

When working as a two component adhesive a pot life of 4 hours must be considered. After 4 hours a portion of up to 4% hardener can be added again in case that the adhesive mix didn't use up. Glue mix which has not consumed in between additional 4 hours has to be disposed. As a rule, do not mix more adhesive as you need for 4 hours working.

E COSTICK 1C (and 2C)

HAVE BEEN TESTED UNDER CONDITIONS AND AGING TESTS IN EUROPE AND ASIA WICH ARE PART OF MODULE 9.

07. Water based sole attaching glue

Answers to often asked questions

How to know the requested durability of a bond?

Heavy footwear, Army, Mountaineering, Athletic Footwear — 2C

"Brown" men shoes (normal street shoes)
Children shoes
Lady shoes
"Brown" shoes — 1C

Winter time with temperatures below 0°C:

The adhesive is damaged when frozen.

Storing conditions

10° - 30°C

Self life

6 months from date of production. After that period the glue has somewhat lower performance due to Hydrolysis.

Application

By brush or machine with rotating brush. Both technologies need brush cleaning in more or less time intervals.

Drying:

Drying time is dependent on the substrates to be bonded and can be supported by heated tunnels or other drying equipment. Anyway, the adhesive film must be glass clear dried to have the best bonding results.

07. Water based sole attaching glue

Answers to often asked questions

Heat activation temperature

The capsulated hardener in the 1 component version starts crosslinking at 70°C. See also sole attaching manual. The 2C version needs a minimum activation temperature of 55°C. Cross linker acts already at room temperature.

Tack and hot tack life

The glue is excellent and so that the assembling of the soles, including spotting and pressing, can be done in a proper way.

Initial strengths

Is high and after a certain pressing time no film stringening should appear. In hot areas with very high outside temperatures and when hard soles or soles not fitting with the upper or soles with very high fight back properties have to be bonded a longer pressing time helps.

Bonding Technology

Describes the different steps of binding shoe substrates together. It includes all steps like substrates preparation, pretreatment steps and necessary products (see also example "shoe manufacturing in Asia")

Capped Capsulated Hardener

Drying time is dependent on the substrates to be bonded and can be supported by heated tunnels or other drying equipments. Anyway, the adhesive film must be glass clear dried to have the best bonding results.

07. Water based sole attaching glue

Answers to often asked questions

Fungi, Yeast, Molds etc.

The adhesive is protected against the attacks of a.m.

Technical Data Sheet (TDS)

Contains some important information regarding physical parameters of a product. See attached SDS for ECOSTICK 1820 1K.

Material Safety Data Sheet (MSDS)

Contains important information regarding possible danger of a product. See attached MSDS for Ecostick 1820 1K.

Milage

The consumption of a water based PUD versus solvent based PUR is much lower. The dry content of PUD is 50%, solvent based have 20%. Hence the PUD's consumption is about 30 – 40% only.

07. Water based sole attaching glue

Adhesive systems

E. The ideal Adhesive Bonds

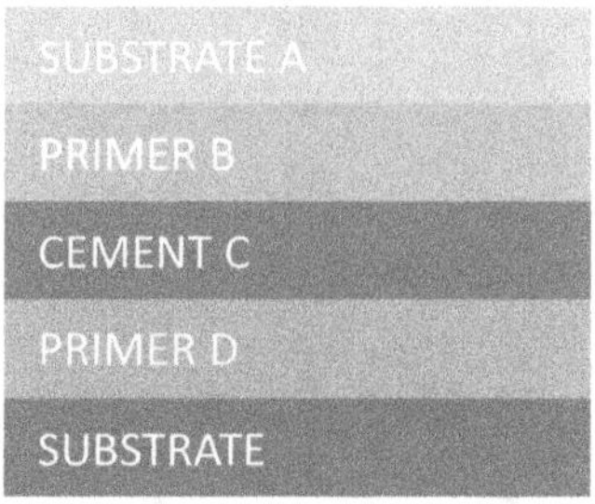

Ideal bonding conditions:
AA=AB=BC=CC=
CD=DE=E
The bond is only as strong as the weakest link.
Just as a chain link.

F. Mode of failure

Cement peel off from substrate side.

Reasons:

- Wrong primer used
- The surface is not well cleaned or buffed (primer applied on the oil surface...)
- Primer is not activated (e.g. UV primer is not passed)

07. Water based sole attaching glue

Adhesive systems

F. Mode of failure
Substrate failure

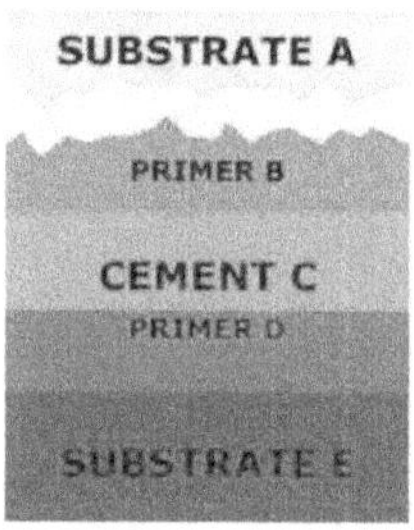

Reasons:

- Best adhesive system can achieve
- Material is too weak, if the bonding is not up to standard

F. Mode of failure
Substrate is slightly peeled off

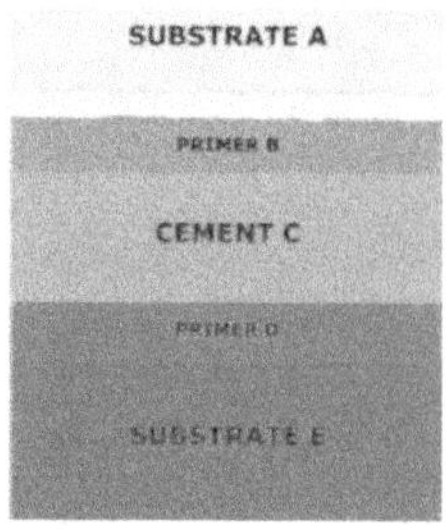

Reasons:

Buff is not proper (leather)

- Primer is not well penetrated (leather primer)
- Substrate is too old (e.g. RB stored too long)

07. Water based sole attaching glue

Adhesive systems

F. Mode of failure

Both sides have cement

For best adhesive bonding results

Get:

- Substrate supplier
- Adhesive supplier
- Application equipment supplier
- Shoe designer

Reasons:

- Cement too dry, or not dry
- Attach the material when cement is cold (wait too long)
- Poor pressing

08. Control mechanism, failure mode, documentation of results

The quality of a bond is also influenced by control of technology, failure mode, control of technology steps.

About this module

Module 8 shows you so-called checklist which can be used for the sole-attaching process, both for the adhesive and the technology, it explains failure modes of the bond, and the peel strengths by using a test machine or a simple hand pincer....

Learning target

- You should know the activities of a quality manager, a testing lab and a production leader...
- The parameter which are important during adhesive application.
- A formula for documentation.
- You should know the ABC of failure modes.

08. Control mechanism, failure mode, documentation of results

Check list

Question	Answer
Adhesive is used in between self life	Yes, see label
Adhesive is mixed up	Yes, 5 minutes
Is upper preparation done properly?	Yes, according substrates
Is the lasting margin large enough?	Yes, 8 -10 mm
Is the adhesive/ Primer applied even?	Yes, no "lakes"
Is the drying time sufficient?	Yes, adhesive film is glass clear and not milky
In case of leather is the roughening done properly?	Yes, penetration of adhesive into leather fibers is okay.

Question	Answer
Is the sole preparation done properly? PUR, PVC, EVA, TPR	Yes, see preparation of soles.
How old are prepared soles?	According minimum drying and longest storing time rules
Is the heat activation of adhesive film sufficient?	Yes, 1 component 70°C 2 component minimum 50°C
Is the pressing of heated soles done when they are warm?	Yes, in between the hot tack life of the glue (1 comp. Approx. 2 min.)
Is the pressing power sufficient?	Yes, according softness/ hardness of soles.
Does midsole and upper fit together?	Yes
Is the pressing power even?	Yes, can be checked with indigo paper.
Is the pressing time long enough?	Yes, minimum 6-8 seconds.

08. Control mechanism, failure mode, documentation of results

Peel strength

All larger Footwear manufacturers have their own system to file the results of peel strengths tested boots.

The peel strengths can be done either by machine or simply by hand, using a pincer.

The documentation should include adhesive/ Primer system, technology of bonding, failure mode and strengths (in case of machine testing) in N/cm.

For own purposes a simple documentation follows:

08. Control mechanism, failure mode, documentation of results

Manual peel strengths test

Client:	Date:
Assembly line:	Adhesive on upper:
Name of shoe:	Adhesive on sole:
Upper material:	Pretreatment of soles:
Soling material:	Setting time:

Evaluation of peel strengths

	Left shoe	Right shoe
a	a. Toe	
b	b.	
c	c.	
d	d. Heel	

Failure mode:________________________________

See manual of sole attaching

Reasons when bond failed:____________________

Results: Passed or failed

09. Test methods, profile of request on WB attaching glues

The requests on a bond must be defined and be able to be reproduced by test method...

About this module

Module 9 gives an overview regarding the different test methods and aging processes. It is clear that lady brown shoe do not need the same requests which have for instance fire fighting, mountaineering or military shoes. Whether a bond is resistant on oil, acids or anti-static or conductive, high heat resistant and high hydrolysis resistant, for all those requests there are test methods and norms.

Learning target

- What are the requests on initial peel strengths
- What are the requests on minimum peel strengths
- What tells us the hydrolysis test?
- What kind of aging tests are additional in use?
- What tells us the creep test? And so on...

09. Test methods, profile of request on WB attaching glues

What kind of stresses can we identify on a bonded sole?

09. Test methods, profile of request on WB attaching glues

ECOSTICK 1 C (and 2 C)

Have been tested under the following conditions and aging tests in Europe and Asia.

	Test	Method	Unit	Standard	Tolerance
1.	Initial peel strength 5 minutes Rubber>rubber (1)		daN/cm	2.5	Minimum
2.	Peel strength 24 hours Rubber>rubber (1)		daN/cm	4.0	Minimum 4.0 for rubber to rubber
3.	Peel strength 5 days Rubber>canvas (1) Rubber>PVC (1+2) Rubber>IMEVA (1+3)		daN/cm	6.0 4.0	Minimum 6.0 for rubber to canvas, Rubber to rubber, and rubber to PVC. 4.0 for rubber to IMEVA
4.	Hydrolysis Peel strength Rubber>Canvas (1) (7 days @ 50°C@ 95% R.H.)		daN/cm % retained daN/cm	5.0 85.0 3.2	Minimum Minimum Minimum
5.	Water immersion Peel strength Rubber>Canvas (1)		daN/cm % retained	5.0 85.0	Minimum Minimum

09. Test methods, profile of request on WB attaching glues

ECOSTICK 1 C (and 2 C)

Have been tested under the following conditions and aging tests in Europe and Asia.

	Test	Method	Unit	Standard	Tolerance
6.	Heat-aging Peel strength Rubber to Rubber (1) (7 days @ 60 ̊C)	According Adhesive Industry	daN/cm % retained	5.0 85.0	Minimum Minimum
7.	Creep resistance Rubber>rubber (1) 70 ̊C, 1.5kg load, 10 min.	According Adhesive Industry	mm	10.0	Maximum
8.	Creep resistance Rubber>rubber (1) 60 ̊C, 2.0 kg load, 10 min.	According Adhesive Industry	mm	10.0	Maximum
9.	Pink stain	According Adhesive Industry	N/A	No stain	--
	Fungi resistance	Internal	N/A	No growth	N/A

1. ... Halogenated   2. ... cleaner MEK   3. ... UV PRIMER

09. Test methods, profile of request on WB attaching glues

Frequently asked questions

Question	Answer
Are 1 component adhesive with capped hardener equivalent in performance with 2 component adhesives?	After heat is applied, a similar performance can be obtained. Important to reach >70°C film temperature. Comparable with a 2C glue with 3% crosslinker
What does crosslinker improve?	Crosslinker improves, among other things, the resistance against heat, hydrolysis, oil, fat, acid and aging performance.
Why should we add outside crosslinker for heavy Footwear/bonding?	Adding outside crosslinker increases heat, hydrolysis and other aging resistance. Heavy footwear has highest requests on aging.
What happens when the heatreactivation is not 70°C?	Crosslinking does not start.

09. Test methods, profile of request on WB attaching glues

Frequently asked questions

Question	Answer
Has one side/two side heat activation an influence?	Yes, one side should reach 80 – 90°C, two side 70°C as a minimum rule. Both upper and sole adhesive films must be able to reach 70°C for crosslinking start
What happens when adhesive is not dry?	Bonding will fail. Adhesive film should be glass clear and not milky.
What happens when crosslinking does not start due to lower activation temperature?	Performance completely uncrosslinked is like a good 1 component PU or CR glue. Performance 1C with adequate heat activation is similar to a 2C glue with 3% crosslinker.

10. Why water based adhesives replace solvent based glues? Health protection; working hygiene, solvent versus water

Fire danger, explosion danger, ozone depleting due to VOC's, ground water pollution, hazardous waste....these are some of the topics when we talk about solvents....

Now we will have a particular look at the role of a safety manager regarding health protection and working place evaluation **WHEN WORKED WITH SOLVENTS**....after that we have plenty of good reasons to change to water based...

Module 10 shows some rules which the legislation powers have set.

Learning target

- Legislation targets
- What are solvents?
- Threshold limit values.
- Ventilation
- Gloves
- Working place evaluation, etc.

10. Why water based adhesives replace solvent based glues? Health protection; working hygiene, solvent versus water

- Legislation powers have set up guidelines on the handling of adhesives containing solvents as regards health Protection and fire prevention as well as the disposal of waste.

- The threshold limit values are an important means of measuring the amount of air pollution permitted from factories. These limiting values state the maximum allowed concentration of pollution in the air which are permitted, so that the demands for pleasant working conditions can be met.

- These threshold limit values are constantly being checked and adjusted where necessary.

- The limits are usually set for a temperature of 20°C with a barometer reading of 760 torr, either in cm3/m3 (cubic centimeter of pure fumes per cubic meter air, according to the American value of ppm = parts per million) or mg/m3 (milligram per cubic meter air).

The maximum concentration limits in the workshop may not be exceeded!!

---

10. Why water based adhesives replace solvent based glues? Health protection; working hygiene, solvent versus water

Physical and chemical properties of solvents

The common solvents in their purest form are water-like liquids, which are lighter than water. The vapours of the solvents are heavier than the air, and the density of the vapours, on a scale of air = 1, lies approx. Between 1 and 6.

Boiling point of common solvents	Evaporation rate (ether = 1) is:
Ethyacetate- 77°C Acetone- 56°C MEK- 80°C	Ethyacetate- 2,9 Acetone- 2,0 MEK- 3,3

10. Why water based adhesives replace solvent based glues? Health protection; working hygiene, solvent versus water

Protection against solvent vapours

The best means of protection is to keep the solvent vapours down to a safe level – to the threshold limit values. These values are gained from experience up to now, or from results of animal experiments which have been carried out over a long time.

These values are to be seen as safety limits of the quality of the air which is inhaled in workshops where the adhesive is used. These limits have been established to mark out the absolute maximum levels and lower values should be aimed for. Apart from that, it is also to be borne in mind that these limits have been set for people of normal health, constitution and sensitivity.

Ventilation: In practice, because of the fact that solvent vapours are heavier than air, they can be exhausted from the air with an appropriate exhausting device, in the direction from ceiling to floor.

For specific health and body protection, the following two points must be noted:

- When using adhesives, smoking must be prohibited (not only because of the danger of fire, since even with a non-inflammable solvent an extremely toxic substance can be produced through heat).
- The storage or consumption of food whilst using solvent based adhesives should also be prohibited. Solvents can dissolve in the fats thus giving rise to the danger that they can be consumed by the mouth with the food.

10. Why water based adhesives replace solvent based glues? Health protection; working hygiene, solvent versus water

Threshold Limit Values

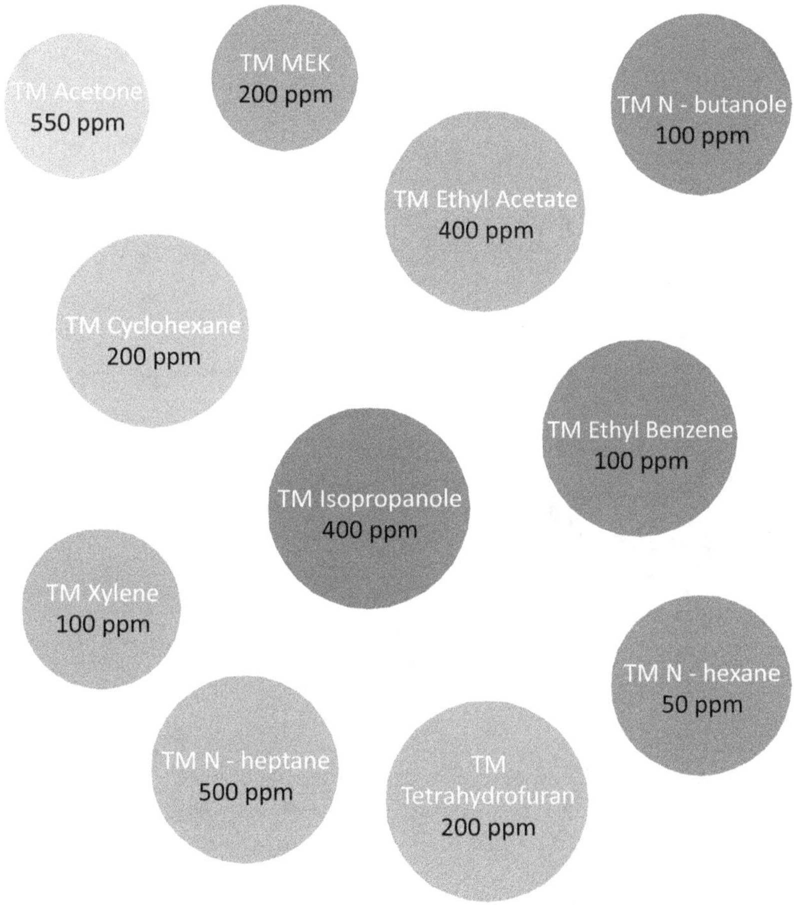

10. Why water based adhesives replace solvent based glues? Health protection; working hygiene, solvent versus water

Effects of solvents on the skin-which health impairments occur from solvents

Solvents can dissolve some amounts of fats. When a solvent comes into contact with skin, the natural fatty protective layer can be destroyed, leading to skin diseases. If this contact is very often, as an example when using a solvent as a skin cleansing lotion. As well as this, this destruction of fat makes it easier for other skin irritation substances to take hold and cause skin changes. It must also be noted that when solvents are allowed to soak into large areas of skin, reabsorbing poisoning is possible.

Let's go a little deeper into the subject of skin damage:

- As in every other profession, the people working in the shoe factory also come in contact with a whole list of substances which could lead to skin damages.
- On the one hand, the more chemical substances that are used, the easier the work becomes, but on the other hand, the bigger possibility is that one of the many shoemakers develops a skin disease because of one of the many substances.

10. Why water based adhesives replace solvent based glues? Health protection; working hygiene, solvent versus water

Three basic types of skin disease can be discussed

There are harmful substances which, because of their chemical components and their tendency to irritate the skin of almost everybody who comes into contact with the substances enough, lead to skin damages.

Such a harmful reaction is called a compulsory toxic reaction, *i.e.* toxic dermatitis.

Secondly,

There are certain substances, which if they are used over a long period of time, even if small concentration can lead to skin damage, can destroy the natural defense and protective bodies which are usually present in the skin, can dry out the skin and can cause cracks thus preparing the way for infections and oversensitive skin. Such skin damage is called erosive dermatitis, *i.e.* a degenerating eczema.

Such substances are for example soaps, in the modern detergents in washing powders, alcohol, gasoline and other fat dissolving substances, as well as alkaline substances such as sodium hydroxide.

10. Why water based adhesives replace solvent based glues? Health protection; working hygiene, solvent versus water

Three basic types of skin disease can be discussed

Thirdly,

the most important group – the so-called allergic eczema or contact eczema. This means that through skin contact with certain substances, the forming of antibodies in the skin occurs so that when the substance comes in contact with this patch of skin again, an "allergic reaction" takes place which turns into eczema.

Here again, there are substances which can lead to such oversensitivity very easily. For example formaldehyde, terpentine, chromium salts and there are others which seldom or never cause such reactions.

- In the particular case of the use of solvents, all three kinds of skin damage can arise.
- The erosive dermatitis is caused by extremely strong cleansing agents which are sometimes used to clean heavily soiled hands and this often gives rise to skin damage.
- This is usually the case when inadequate, *i.e.* skin irritating cleansing agents are used, for example gasoline, paraffin, and when these liquids are not properly rinsed off or when the skin is not regressed afterwards with a protective skin cream.

10. Why water based adhesives replace solvent based glues? Health protection; working hygiene, solvent versus water

Three basic types of skin disease can be discussed

- Oversensitivity of the skin can eventually be caused by chromium tanned leather for example, because chromium is a substance which can very easily lead to irritation.

- On the same line, some rubber material that is used can also lead to such eczemas whereby the damage is caused not only by the rubber alone, but also by the substances contained in the rubber, such as colour pigments, protective agents against ageing or plasticizers.

- Such skin damage appears not only amongst people who actually make or repair shoes, but also amongst the shoe wearers, who can also suffer from skin irritation, on the feet.

- Very generally, it can be said that people with certain skin deficiencies, *i.e.* inherited skin abnormalities are more likely to develop oversensitive skin than normal healthy people.

- This group includes people such as those with Ichthyosis, with overactive sebaceous glands or people with particular kinds of eczema.

10. Why water based adhesives replacing solvent based glues? Health protection; working hygiene, solvent versus water

Protective measures against absorption of harmful substances into the skin

It is very important that all those working with these modern adhesives follow various safety regulations:

1. The adhesive processes should be carried out in the special place provided for them, which have been specially prepared and equipped according to strict hygienic regulations.
2. If necessary use of protective gloves
3. Use of protective skin cream before beginning adhesive process will help.
4. After work, hands should be cleansed with an appropriate paste, whereby patches of adhesive on the skin can be removed with crepe or ethyl acetate. After thoroughly rinsing with water, hands should be regressed with a protective cream.

10.Why water based adhesives replace solvent based glues? Health protection; working hygiene, solvent versus water

Protective measures against absorption of harmful substances into the skin

It is absolutely necessary to have an adequate knowledge on how "clean" the solvents in use are.

- Are we sure, that e.g. special grade of petroleum spirit does not contain benzene or n-hexane?
- Are we sure that if toluene is used, the quality is not contaminated with benzene?

Please remember:

- There are solvents which do not have any threshold limit values. Basically this means that even smallest portions can impair health. One example therefore is benzene.
- Even a trace of benzene cannot be tolerated and therefore it is important to assure the use of "clean solvents".

10. Why water based adhesives replace solvent based glues? Health protection; working hygiene, solvent versus water

A clever safety manager at a factory

Observes the following facts:

- Toxic and certain physical properties of solvents: vapor pressure, evaporation speed, heat of evaporation, density.
- Local condition at the working place: size and shape of the working rooms, ventilation, climatic requirements.
- Technical condition for spreading: application methods, adhesive consumption per unit of time.
- Technical assessment of work: degree of exertion (e.g. physical work load is closely related to the amount of solvent vapours which are absorbed), other people present on the workplace.

10. Why water based adhesives replacing solvent based glues? Health protection; working hygiene, solvent versus water

A clever safety manager at a factory

Observes the following facts:

Therefore the safety inspectors for the workplaces had to take into consideration any eventual physical strain whilst work was carried out and had then set the limit values of solvent vapor concentration according to his findings. For this, he could start with the fact that for normal work strain, the hygienic safety limits apply to about 15 liters per minutes of air which is inhaled.

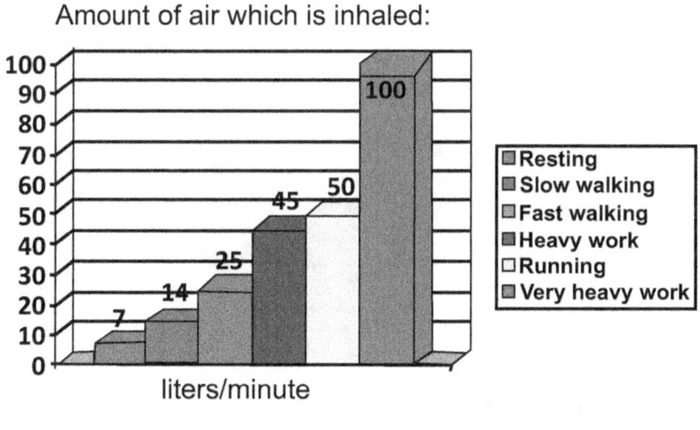

www.ingramcontent.com/pod-product-compliance
Lightning Source LLC
Chambersburg PA
CBHW062111160726
48282CB00026B/761
9789390479948